MW01537493

This Journal Belongs to

Published by

Real Joy Publications

Made in the USA
Las Vegas, NV
14 December 2021

37859673R00069